We See Nothing

Poems By

Nick Boyer

ISBN: 978-81-962026-2-0

First Edition: 2023
Rs. 200/-

Cyberwit.net
HIG 45 Kaushambi Kunj, Kalindipuram
Allahabad - 211011 (U.P.) India
http://www.cyberwit.net
Tel: +(91) 9415091004
E-mail: info@cyberwit.net

Printed at VCORE.

Contents

We See Nothing

After Gwendolyn Brooks

We so cool
in the cool breeze
of eternal recess
in the rainbow cesspool
beyond space further than
the wall, facing the tapestry

The drunken stool
we need nothing
atop the next worse soul
we aid each other
linking arm in arm
going sideways
never up

The holy fool
in the classroom
at either end of
every spectrum
you will never be noticed
what a shame

Nothing in All

In this steady, complacent, ascent,
I see sitting participants,
The ones Whitman saw on his ride across the water,
The individuals he saw,
Remain in a different sense,
A new sense,
In a real sense,
So deep in our origins it now presents itself as a new idea.

In this steady, complacent, ascent,
I see God,
Several authors,
Crafting stories of legend,
Reaching for myth while God rests in their ribcages,
Aching for flesh,
But forcibly crafted a deity.

In this steady, complacent, ascent,
I see my pixelated reflection,
It takes the shape of an odd poem that doesn't make much sense.

In this steady, complacent, ascent,
I see no dreams and hold my breath during the day,
I hate the reflection I see,
Walking past me on the streets.

Hello?

Is this
    Searching?
Is existence enough and is a conviction to be regarded?
If so,
    Please come out.

I look for you in the streets,
On the concrete, on the shop side of the street, with ethnic smells at each block, with shopping carts on the road,
Out my window, when I'm blinded and only see spotty pigments that dance,
When I wiggle my fingers above the keys, after I smile, and before I cry.

Come out, ripe seed!
Come out, illuminated self!
Come out, and hand me the scroll!

I look for you in my pulsating skull,
I see
    (I think I see)
Your shadow in my blurred vision,
I hear
    (I think I hear)
Your voice ringing in my ears.

I feel your embrace in my chest full of spasms, and
Your kiss when my eyes water, and
Your elation when I sweat beneath cold covers,

Your cool fingers when I undress -
    I write with the seams of my shirt torn in the back.

Come out, reflection!
Come out, eager referee!
Come out, and hand me the rulebook!

I am everywhere at once,
But have never been in your presence,
We have known each other an eternity,
What an indifferent host you are!

You bloodied my test paper,
But I return,
Always,
As I am, and
Who I will be,
So you will smell my scent when I have quit,
All I ask,
Is to put a name to your face,
A face to your feeling,
A feeling to your sense,
A sense of your reason,
A reason for your cause,
    Then I will follow suit.

The Tiny Woman in the Sky

The highest I can see,
I call the divine,
I see just past Her neck,
Enough to see Her ocean-pebble pupils,
    The torn and blind stones,
And the teetering scales that lay upon each of Her palms,
The divine
That knows all,
And the one I judge,
As the animals judge me,
And as the plants judge the animals.

I cry wrongdoing at Her
When my dog runs away from home,
Or when pollen sifts between my eyelids,
    The
    small things.

    The
small things,
A mangled spirit that shares my bed,
A constant motion within that has no direction,
A blank sheet with no traumatic ink,
A closed mind that thinks too highly of itself,

Life and
Death,
    The
    small things,

I cry with a mouthful of rain,
Begging her to swing the ever-wavering scales,
And hold still.

The Lights Went Out

Last night I think the lights went out, I think I flipped the switch and it broke -

No, I saw it -

I know it happened,

The lights went out,

It was all obsidian,

It was so elating,

To not feel,

Then it was so distant,

It was almost doughy, everything was made from the clay of life, and it was still moldable.

The lights went out, so I grabbed binoculars.

The lights went out, so I burned a book.

The lights went out, so I hid beneath the covers and accepted the new Earth.

After the lights went out,

I forgot to care when you told me what no other ears ever heard,

My kin became a framed photo,

I relied on shaky hands,

I became sick whenever I lost the back of my eyelids,

I won an Oscar and thanked myself at the podium,

I took a nap

Just so I could crave once more,

And stare at my toes for a bit.

Thank You for the Mask

There was screaming and there were threats -
    All that the ceiling covered was wrong -
Fuses sparked and crossed beneath my undeserving crown -
    The wounds never healed, for they were never exposed to air -
After the dishes shattered, the floor panels started to come up.

I forgot because I wanted to,
Because I wanted to be brave,
    I am... I am...
Because of the mirror where the window should be,
Because that is who we are.

I was brave,
I stood up when the roof caved in, and
Turned down the thermostat when I saw a frigid corpse across from me.

I think I want to say
    Thank you,
When I turned my back on you,
And you followed,
Weapon in hand,
My feet froze once the dew-coated night grass of fall swallowed them,
And I howled,
Then I never wanted to be brave again,
Never wanted to be called to action again,

So,

Thank you,
For this mask,
I know it cost you nothing, but
Thank you.

I, a Citizen

Now it is spring,
    It does not matter what is out of the
                                        Window,
When I lay down these words,
It is spring,
When I somersault in an office chair,
It is spring,
When I read Ginsberg and feel panic,
I feel rushed, I feel lesser,
It is spring,
When this next line arrives…

I have seen nothing in any sidewalk reflection, in any distant belittled,
    A harsh judge,
I am
A solution of sanity,
    Of reality,
            Out the window,
I am there, roasting pork in the streets,
Making Chicken Kyiv,
    (there is a brawl in the alleyway)
Going home and bathing naked,
Bathing in created scenes,
The prior life, and
The next one.

A few stars lay at my feet,
The clouds are at my nose,

Drowning & Flying,
Floating & Falling.

In my cave below the water, follow me,
Follow me, there are hermits with degrees and a homeless mayor,
(He can see, we are blind)
Here I am neutral,
A learning prophet
Who is unemployed.

Maybe
Next time I peer out the window, standing on my toes,
I will fall out
And then be inspired,
For I am not like the mayor,
I need a roof -
But no roof is needed in spring.

It won't be spring again -
Not until it is spring forever.

Walk Home

Port wine secretes from the blinds of my face.
With each stride the indolent world warps and washes, leaving ground-born suds of cotton to form thin layers of dough in the pie of life.
The silk-blue minions pass me on my right,
The wise and unfortunate alluring rapport that could slip through budding molecules, and still they are denied (I deny it, but so does my reflection in the street), passed me on my left.
Spikes in the heel of Earth's core are to be avoided, and, oh, the masses acquiesce in their decision to march.

I see a tiger striped half-and-half: one a seam of the constellations and one a waxy white.
I see a giraffe with garden snakes circling its neck like a barbershop pole.
I see flattened and gray jungle grass that is Ted-Bundy-VW-Bug-yellow and tinted with bourbon stains.
I see a half-skinned raccoon with eclipse pupils in the shop glass reflection.

Squishy concrete pulls at my toes like dank sand beneath a parting tide and my steps are muddy.
In my boots - the one thing separating me from the rest - it is an unlit hand-dug hole in the amazon;
Tigers and giraffes lurk in the grass.
I slap the back of my neck after a city-fairy nips at my neck and the flood damn splinters, inviting chunks of rock to act as ornaments while I am on holiday.

My speaker keeps a cheery tune about drowning on a loop;
I would feel so light then, and we would all drown in an expanse
of rolling fur-ridden waves that reflect a cave-dwelling rainbow.

Arable Sky/Love

When I look up through the window,
    From a
        Seated
    Position,
I see the gray bubble I lay within;
A swirling oyster that fends off the light.
The end and the beginning,
And I lay in the middle, with you by my
                    Side.

If I stare long enough,
The gray sky turns white,
    Illuminating,
    The womb of a pearl.
    I see strings of LSD when I blink,
Then back to gray.

You live in the dark with a single bulb atop your head.
It was fried by the time I woke,
By the time the sky was gray,
By the time we were entombed by vapor.

When I stand, it is all worse:
    I see where you can hide, where you can be lost.
    A chill spins me around and all I see is barren land
        (The bulb is too dim).
    I find you asleep,
Somehow that is worse:

I see where you can be found,
But the concrete interrupts my expedition.

Perhaps,
You are a child of the soil.
And perhaps,
I
Am supposed to garden.

List: Why I Love You

Because you force yourself to be silent when the pitch-black looks too succulent and desirable.
Because I swelter and smolder the carpet with each step when the slightest water droplet lands on my ear.
Because, now, the entire day will be silent and on edge and full of slammed doors, and it is only morning.
Because halfway through our grocery trip you left to sit in the car.
Because when you are one with the damp and dull morning air, you know you cannot talk to me, and I hate that.
Because I love you always, but only consider it went it is silent and you are a room away.
Because I watch you each day - I keep a journal - and imitate my art.
Because I am scared of heights, yet we live at the top of a skyscraper, our legs always dangling over the toy city.
Because you like it hot and I like it cold, and as a result, the thermostat is broken.
Because the road under construction is still quicker than the detour - at least the foreman says so.
Because hound dogs don't hunt anymore and cats hate the front yard grass.
Because cloudy days bring the least trouble.
Because the effects of liquor have not been quantified within the apartment walls, but we call ourselves mad scientists at night, sometimes in the afternoon.
Because what is better than this? Maybe something, but it only exists outside the window, so nothing is better than this.
Because we are real, and together we don't have to hide it.
Because the next day you will change the sheet and we can hide

behind the eyes of slumber.
Because I need to feel important.
Because I change to another tab while I write and you pass behind me.
Because the fuzzies are swarming my peeled-open eyelids, but I can't find the utopian village of words.
Because that does not matter; I am your favorite poet when I am drunk on the couch.

Time with you makes me write

Jogging ivory hills pace below my dry palm. Smooth trail, a destination of nothing, a beautiful nothing. No more chase. No more worry. Reality eludes the wet cloth of a venom-spun silk cradle, where the water never changes pace and our legs only wobble when we desire. It is a puddle of the stars behind our eyelids. It is safe. Iron-spined with cushion muscles and rubber tendons. It is Venus and fresh air and forest dew on an Upstate morning at the break of Autumn. It is beyond us. Beyond us together. Third-person perspective would leave us in the same awe. Murderous temptation is indifferent - we play with the corpses. We write Epics and forget how they began when our eyes open. Curse sunsets and yell, *Holy!* once the cowardly sun has left. No distraction. No focus. Honey-soaked limbs. Still hearts. Still. Hearts. In unison. Under one God. We found the lord beneath the ceiling and decided he could stay. We erase trauma and mute past arguments with just a stumbling fall. Together. Earlier I threw the printer out the window. Later we need more ink (pick up at the Blood Drive). Now. We write. Poetry. Flesh and pen and blood and ink. Never to be released. Who would understand? Comprehend? Not even the ceiling knows. Though it might see. It doesn't know. The walls don't know what they contain. The neighbors cannot live in solitude long as we breathe. The city will burn if we leave. We will set flame to the street if we stay. But now, where cold and hot are unknown and dismissed, it can wait. All of it. There will be another Ice Age before we shiver - or even dress. Only for a moment - a moment long as we desire - I am comfortable.

What the jug of port wine sees while it is being murdered

It's a shitty life but it's my life. I am born, sold, sold again, then killed. They can recycle my corpse, but once I am drained of blood, that's it.

I am glad to be of service. This couple seems like they are having fun.
I think they love each other. I think this is beautiful.

They laugh a lot. They are starting to speak louder, but I don't mind. I'm getting a little dizzy, but there are worse ways to go - I'd assume.

The room's air is beginning to feel fuzzy. Someone said something and the other replied, slightly louder, but they are still interested in me.

They are still loud but not laughing. One moved to another couch. The floor shakes when they walk toward me. I am beginning to feel nauseous.

What are they doing? Why are they angry? Did I do this?
I feel light. They keep eyeing me and choking me. It won't be much longer.

One says that they will pour me out. The other says I have done nothing for them.
They both grab me again anyways, at separate intervals. It's quiet now.

One left the room. The other started to beat the keyboard. I am on my deathbed.
They know no mercy, no bounds, no love. They only know doubt and death.

I heard one begin to cry. The other beat on the keyboard harder.
They breathed hard. I was scared when they stormed by.

One begged the other to stop crying, then the other cried louder.
One yelled
then marched by me again and I felt my stomach churn as I shook with each thud.

Just kill me. I feel gray and I hate it here. I think the angry one looked at me;
please, please kill me. Stomp around one more time, strangle me, and

put me out of my misery. My life has little to offer,
but I prefer my existence to what I have seen before me.

Now it is dark and I am weak.
I have been shown no mercy and I must suffer another night.

you asked why I love you

Green stage
Ripe curtain
Us
on the bench
You
shifting spots
The sun
is in your eyes
Nicotine-soaked
lips
reaching
like an ax-pick
for a dusty mountain's summit
Silence
hums
Outweigh
the thruway
Babies
on leashes
Dogs
in strollers
Old men
Riding bikes
Ignoring
us
I cross
and re-cross
my legs
Remind me

to allow some air to the
round
silver
ink-spoiled
brain
You
at ease with silence
that is mountainous
to me
Flys
cause self-harm
and itching
I finally have
an answer
for you
:
I never
would tell my mom
I loved her
until I said it to you.

Everything and less

Chuckles dry as a skinned knee on a desert road.
Sleep that is a dream of what death could feel like,
and yet I know it is not so. A knot in my neck that feels
like a wilted grapevine, frail and failing; the scent of
screaming grapes run in zig-zags beneath my nose,
tickling my cheeks and laughing all the while.
Leathery blocks that numb my ass, but I guess I like
it because I don't stand. Pinballs in my chest, a fuzzy
blanket of organs, quick jabs that end at the tip of my
throat. Mini-me is choosing a secure gate to strut
along a calender, slipping on a Tuesday, head falling
on a Sunday. Mechanical eyes and stray tree-crumb
fingertips, producing defective products perfectly.
Whitewashed brick eyeballs veined with angel-hair
font graffiti: *keep writing*. Zombie-crawling to the
blanketed cradle and pouring my heart into a pint glass.
Speaking in tongues to a steak knife and calling it dinner.
Scribbled on paper, written in pen, erased with rubber,
and burned at the stake. Face-to-face with a window
pane, convincing myself I feel the heavy ocean breeze
sap my skin. I see my bleached reflection, the
loose-pebble liquid that freckles my face - since
I just ran the dishwasher. Enbowed lenses that
fishbowl capsized perception; I see myself bound in
jelly-cotton that only hides, all day and all night.
All within God's footstep, rays of light live and cease
and blur into cylindrical pandemonium, when clocks
sound and scheduled love is made. All within a day.

We Can

We could go downtown
And call the lighters streetlights.
We tell ourselves
That we can smell the ocean
From this dark concrete corner.

We can always throw
The steak back on the grill, but
Do not char the meat.
I will go to the butcher;
I am familiar there.

We can add gas too,
Watch the building sacrifice
Itself. We will know
The cause and beauty of the
Material Inferno.

We can play with sharp
Knives whilst we raise warm glasses,
Bleeding hand-in-hand.
Look at the night sky and stars:
It is what we desire.

It is who we are.
Kaos and flames and wild tears,
But then love. Then, love.
Always love and always yes.
There is no other option.

It is a clear sky.
That is what we say at night,
In loose harmony.
Know that I don't pity you.
I hope you don't pity me.

Work It Out

There's a greasy leather bench and I chose another so I didn't have to wipe it down. I came straight from labor to labor so I was slicked in salty sins and tired of what the day cursed me with.

1 2 3 4

And Louie texted me - I noticed because my AirPod fell out of my ear and I shook my head in disgust - asking if I wanted to smoke, which sounds generous on his part but wasn't because I had the weed and not much other money, so I shook my head again. I didn't want to go home and have Louie over, not because I don't like him, but because *why* the house was empty. The iron grip of the weights stretched and burned my palms.

1 2 3 4

We will be back by tonight, my parents said. Come on, Louie said. Commercial grunts spiral my earlobes. Do I look like I am losing weight? The mirror is indecisive. Tennis shoes squeak some read on Kindles others fall in love with themselves. I wondered who was thinking that about me. What makes me so great?

1 2 3 4

I was going to regardless of whether I responded to my dear friend or not. The water almost tastes dry; I can't differentiate it from my lips. There are a lot of relaxation options here: CNN, Fox News, an adult-sized UV microwave and I hate them all. No one can relax: It looks like a herd of high-quality meat led by uniform visuals: There are a lot of mirrors. I lick my lips for the taste of lukewarm liquidated salt and roll back onto the bench.

A swarm of wasps in my pocket:
Nick, the text read:
Your grandfather has passed away.

Grandpa Cheeseburg'

Next time,
I want my grandfather
To tell the same drugstore counter jokes
For *all* the Christmases.

At his
Funeral, my father said he
Wouldn't want us to be disheartened,
He'd want us to have our own Mardi Gras.

I thought
About the first Blue Light
Swig he gave me on a humid August
Night, the electric buzz of crickets surrounding us.

Next time,
I want to hear the same scratchy
Laugh after each punchline.
To smell the grease-soaked brown-paper-bag

As he
Laughs through the front door and
The dogs' paws clamor against the hardwood,
And their tales wag at his feet.

Rehab in the Cosmos

After this life
Admit me to the white clothes and blue masks
The artificial white light and tiled floors
Wheel me in
Tie my gown in the back, please
Then I will speak through images and toss my stress onto the rest of time
I will tell
    How relations never improved
    How we grew more ignorant
    How advances regressed us
    How *us* doesn't apply to this group
    How we are all lost in a maze of mirrors
    How the words were twisted, translated, picked apart, and rewritten
    How those who had the message were slain before they could speak
    How rosy-cheeked actors were shown to a podium and given a script of agenda-fitting lies
    How the small things became immovable objects that sunk into the Earth
Then I will take a breath and
I will tell
    How I failed
    How they wouldn't listen
    How I was a coward for not trying to snag their ear
    How they never gave me a step
    How my legs were wobbly

How my voice was hoarse
How
I
Failed
So, tell me what to do next
because free will
cost me a life
Admit me to rehab in the cosmos.

Currency

On a guardrail I call a bench -
Dog days of Summer -
The only time to get paid
Working with my hands
Peeling back dollar bills
I can't pick long
So I settle for poems
Because I am a writer
Yes
A man
Yes
A hard-working man of leisure
Ill to effort
Wheeling asphalt
Writing unpublished smear
All labor
All bad
Money is in the midst of this thought
Somewhere
Beneath my fingernails
Between purple ink and the skin of my pinky
Between silence and argument
Somewhere I am
But am not aware of
So I sit and try to familiarize my surroundings

Eulogy

Cover my face, please.
See tomorrow and write it
down. Slit your wrists and

you will be seen. I
am here - tell me now, was the
funeral joyous?

Did the streets stall
with traffic? Did the bomb go
off? How many are

left? Is all wrong now?
Static pulse. Response hangs in
the balance of wind.

The hands ticked once more.
Traffic was light on that night.
The sky was cloudless.

My laptop was not
opened. Poems wilted and
ran off with the wind.

My scar on the skin
of life: faded. I should have
cut deeper. Brought a

larger knife. I should
have murdered life's impression
and burnt the corpse crispy.

I should have waited
and seen tomorrow, for then
I'd have one more chance.

Checked off on my agenda

Abyssal deep-wound waters break the dog's leg with the buzz-off gesture of *my* wrist.
Purple flesh (it looks squishy, like a red blood cell),
skinned without a fight, skinned until it tarnishes, going lifeless into the paper.

Next: make my neck ache. Search for gratitude, turn each moss-befriended rejection of soil.
The labor will be tedious and unrewarding, but afterward, I can feel less until I can become a fossil for a brief eon, then toil with oil-slick pens and Amazon-wet notebooks.

Because boredom is the light swimming through the blinds,
the bedsheets are drawn to a quick tent, and I beg myself to
wake each morning only to circle around the bed like the moon.

It is,
sitting cross-legged on a cone-shaped stone, trying to organize
a solo picnic, and complaining about the wind.

It is,
letting my veins pump for a flash of ink,
alive only when it dies.

It is,
when the edge of a page divides the fragile roof of my
fingertip and I have only one thought: More ink.

Jump

Pale-skinned sky.
Curly wisps of cloud that
are all fingernails. I
see my reflection
at the skyscraper's tip -
erect from industrial fields,
I fondle the city's joy.
Pleasure myself.
Excited blood
will rain around
the same time the
mirror cries and the
shards are
too enticing to
my fingertips.
All ugly, like the clouds
and leaves of grass. Early
onset Rigor Mortis while
I can still see and the
skyscraper still stands
on the cusp of the
gravity. I don't
want to leave.
Life will be
full, for once.
Death
will be dreadful, only
moments before
it arrives.

Four Men and a Dead Car

Four men
push a beat up
junker of a car
through four-lane traffic.

There are collared shirts
seated before minimum
wage plates. There are
families that do not know
each other. There is me,
buzzed on the sidewalk,
not worthy of the action on my T.V.

Whaling car horns circle the
four men like a hawk around a
rat. I didn't know whether I wanted
them to turn the corner or die in
a collision of car parts and intestines.

I laugh at them. The girl beside me
laughs as well. I doubt that is what
the four men wanted: to be laughed at
and harassed. But I suppose that was the
lesser of two evils in their world. Did
they know each other? Were they strangers?
There was no way to tell.

Then they were gone and around
the corner. I followed them and found

an empty street. I don't think anyone
won that night. I went up to my apartment,
looked out the window, and watched the rest play in ignorant
glee.

some tears here and there

Sometimes
when I am alone in this fake, electric space
I think about

All the times I have been shamed for crying.
Once, it was from my grandpa.
Sunday Sauce
after dinner
I was playing football in the yard with my dad.
I fell
thought I got hurt
and started crying.

I asked my grandpa for ice
with tears on my skin.
He said
that I shouldn't cry.

I remember that vividly.
I cannot remember the other moments as well.
They weren't as direct.
They came from family members
friends
and teammates.
They faded and meshed and intertwined
to create a splotch that lives on the lens of my mind.
It is colored like unsure regret.

I still cry.

When I do
I cry twice:
Once for the moment
and
one because I wasn't supposed to cry.

The Window

My affair
With the window
Continues.
She calls my name when
It is silent
When you
Call for me.

The window
Is beautiful
Because it is
Everchanging.
Some days
It is
Gray and aged.
Others,
It is yellow
Like a baby
With jaundice.
Freckled with late
Arrivals, diplomatic can-
Collectors, sidewalk
Inventory producers,
Suited warehouse day-
Shifters.

The window
Knows me
Holds my reflection

In its rigor mortis
Fingertips.
Somewhere
In its sights
The window
Has seen
My last death and
My next birth.

The window
Says I can
See for myself,
All beneath its gaze,
If I lean out and
Dare to fool gravity.

Abundant Rags, We Are Not
Rags of skin
cut and sewn by
all of us
or none of us;
but the rags are equipped
and we dawn them like service ribbons.

Stitched -
at least we assume them to be -
and scarred,
raw and
tired;
these adjectives amount to
a humanity
that cannot find
abundance.

Perhaps,
there is too much beyond the walls
of our skin,
and we weigh too much -
too many twice-used rags -
to reach even a molecule beyond
ourselves
and reach

abundance.

Holding

Onto today, tomorrow, and yesterday.

When I was a young boy I crawled carpets with a plastic hammer in my grip. Once I had a dream an old man with a terrible frown shoved me backward down a green slide with highway traffic below me.

Yesterday I yelled at Her, said the "H" word, and then went for a walk. A trail formed beneath my feet, and soft, white, stringy wishes got caught beneath my feet.

A few years ago I dreamed I tackled an active shooter on campus. The next night I dreamed of my drug dealer chasing me through my suburban neighborhood, firing shots from a pistol; I ran into a neighbor's garage, and when I came out, I killed him with a baseball bat.

My eyes speak in morse code at night, and I am only fluid in sight, so my missions are forgotten, a dead-end is ahead, the brick path is thinning, and the spaces between mortar contain piss-yellow dead grass that only stands to be knocked down.

Perhaps,
Today I will dream of cutting a blade of grass, or
Tomorrow I will smash a brick on the path with a sledgehammer,
because
Yesterday I started down this path.

The Next Bell

It's what I signed up for
in the very end
my lungs will give
and you will see that I was telling the truth:

I couldn't do it;
I couldn't survive
I couldn't figure out how everyone
continued

I learned arithmetic
and safe sex
and enough for framed paper
and how near death is
Now, a new lesson:
the temptation of the end

I am being taught by
stoplights
traffic
shot eyes
a sore back
and the overwhelming void

Last time
the bell rang
it was graduation day

and that is the lesson:
the next bell cannot ring
soon enough.

Dead cat... Poison Apple... Sharp rocks in webbed feet...

Between each frequency, each broadcast and news break
Land of Us... Live and work... Rise early...
Slithering up and around our throats then gauging out our eyes
Flag... Prayer... Family in the house...
Then our intestines go - whatever we have left - and we will seem happier
Sobriety... Drink our water... Eat our food...
No one will be left to recall the days of the past
History... Legacy... We will lead...
When we were so different we unified as one
Division... A plot of land... Work to eat...
This is still the case today, only worse
One life... It is ours... Heaven or Hell...
We are moving toward the end
No rebellion... We are a nation... You are a child...
And no one is aware of the fight
40 hours a week... Night time with your children... Make more soldiers...
Even though the enemy has already spread its web
Seek and destroy... Only one captor... It must all belong to the Fathers...
And we are consumed by our thought-to-be leader.

Mechanical Cat

The mechanical cat inside the Thai Food place
is trying to tell me something. It holds its paw
at a 90-degree angle, then waves it back and
forth. Should I go? Should I fall to my knees?
Hmm - my legs are wobbling.

I asked for a menu; I had never had Thai food.
I got the Pad Thai. The waiter told me to do
it with the shrimp, which I did. I sat down
hard at the booth and waited. The cat's paw
continued to taunt me.

Then I was served. The waiter said I looked
sleepy. I was half drunk. On the street, I saw
a woman fall off an electric scooter. I saw a
cigarette smoker cough and ash a cigarette with
only two hits off it. I saw a homeless man ask
for money and then shake his head.

I haven't seen the hills on the horizon in too long,
I think. I haven't smelt enough and I keep my head
down while I walk, I think.

I think the night's cavalry is bearing down on me,
but maybe no one else notices. I think the outdoors
are toxic and fresh air kills. I think any bottled liquid
is poison, and all the meat has cancer - in and around
the butcher shop. I think the sky is repugnant and I am
equal to a slug while standing on the sidewalk.

Standing on the sidewalk, thinking an unrecorded conversation with myself. Someone is trying to get someone else to confess, but there hasn't been a body found yet. Standing in the parking lot and imagining it as my living room. Standing on the bed, jumping on the mattress like a child, and crying with my alarm. Seeing and hoping my surroundings are as worthless as my bones.

The food was good.
I laid down in bed -
I think that's what
the mechanical cat
wanted. So, I opened
my eyes and began
to write.

Il Gatto

There is a cat rummaging through the dumpster. It is pawing at rancid meat and smoothing crumpled newspapers with its tongue. It nestles against the rusted green base of the dumpster and purs to itself. When the cat sees me it runs away. *No!* I

yell. *Come back!* I wanted the cat to finish its meal; I must be the void of joy. I am here but not surviving - the cat was different. The cat was *here*, unaware of any agenda or force, living for life. Then the cat was gone and I felt I had to go. I had to find something

else. I walked on. No other life allowed my observation, they all passed
by. Everyone and everything passes - I think this as I walk. Then I come
to a stop; the crosswalk light yells at me. I look left then right: no cars. I
scattered across the road like a cat; I rebelled like the cat; I lived like the cat.

The cat knows no emotion only action. Look at me; I cannot even weep when
I want to. I can barely feed myself, let alone my soul. I am not confident
enough to fight. The cat doesn't fear the logistics. I am tripped up by slithering
data that slides up the pantleg of every man, woman, and child on the street.

There has to be something else - I think this as I walk. Then I arrive at my apartment.
I want to turn around but there is traffic. I want to see more but the streets are empty
and there is a rubber eraser in the sky. So I enter the building while cursing my feet.
Everything is calm for a moment. Then I realize there is nothing next and I panic.

What would the cat do?

Little White Dog

You've seen a couple of backyards
and been on a couple of car rides.
Now you circle the living room
blindly, crying creaky stairway whimpers.

I think everyone knows what you are
saying. I do. But no one has the heart
- or lack thereof. I don't. But I do
remember the acute bark you

weren't sure of - the one you learned from
the big dog on the plane. It woke me up,
though I was unsure how, and I thought I
was dreaming. You were in my mom's arms,

as you are tonight. I am your second favorite,
but I understand. Now you can't see the
ground before you, and you don't respond to
your name, but your little nub wiggles when I

dangle my fingertips in front of your wet snout.
When I cradle you against my chest you go limp;
you can't see, but you know I am there. So, I will
write this now, while you know I am here.

Lilly

the 15-year-old
dog,
is now a cold corpse
on the bathroom floor
of my parents' house.

She lived
her last day
in the bathroom -
door locked -
with three dog beds
covering the hardwood
floor,
blind and deaf,
falling over her feeble limbs.

That night,
after work,
I called my mom,
knowing myself
that Lilly wanted
to die.

My mom
had just got back from work
when I called.
She went to check on Lilly
in the bathroom

and discovered
no breath.

A few days ago
I wrote a poem
about Lilly
and how
she was withering away
and how
I was living
on a leash.

Well,
Lilly,
at least
one of us
can walk
freely
now.

Good Girl

The dog puked in the car
once on the way to the grocery store
and once on the way back.

You held the dog
and cleaned up the puke
while I got ground beef and tortillas.

I didn't say anything
just got in the car
and went to a drive-thru.

I waited a while at the window
but then I smiled
and you asked why.

I was thinking of death
I said
then the window opened

and a teenage girl
handed me a greasy
brown paper bag.

I went to hand you the bag
but you were looking out the
window so I set it on your lap.

Eventually you grabbed the bag
when the dog started to poke
around; I guess the dog was still hungry.

I asked what was wrong
and you didn't answer at first
but eventually you spoke

in a broken whisper
and said that you were surrounded
by death your whole life

and that you were trying to
make a change, but I always spoke of
death and suicide.

And I saw where you were coming
from, because I am ungrateful and selfish
and it hurt to sit in the passenger's seat for

a moment. I apologized but that wasn't
enough - it will never be enough. But
your pure soul; you took me back after

only a few minutes. Then we pulled back
into our apartment parking lot and the dog
began gagging on your lap, making strange

faces with its ears pinned back, but you
whipped out a poop bag and brought it to their
face; the dog gagged and retched, and when

they were done my car was spotless. I tossed the
jiggly bag of puke in the dumpster and
we all went into the apartment silently.

I love you and you taught me how

You need to pot the plant
in direct sunlight
but it cannot be overexposed,
and it must get enough water,
but you cannot flood the soil.

You need to fold the page neatly,
crease the edges and smooth it
with your palm. You need to lick
the envelope, but not dampen the material.

You need to guide it down the street,
hand-in-hand, on the inside of the sidewalk,
and not walk too fast, but keep up with the pace.

You need to check its pulse,
even when it is running alongside you,
and fetch water
when its glass is empty.

You need to cut the crust of its sandwiches
and put ice cubes in its soup. You need to
check its temperature, grab prescriptions
when it is ill, and drive it to school when it is faking.

You need to forget yourself
for now
and meet yourself again
when you are just half
of something whole.

Vet Visit

My girlfriend and I adopted a mutt from Puerto Rico.
She got caught up in the last hurricane and they found her
with her three puppies.
Then someone picked her up
and we bought her off them.

From Puerto Rican beaches
to an Upstate New York winter,
but she handles it well;
she shivers but doesn't whine
and I wish I could be more like her.

Today was her first vet appointment
and I was worried.
It took her weeks to warm up to me;
she took to my girlfriend first.
She scurries when we walk by men on the street;
we've concluded that she was beaten by a man
near those Puerto Rican beaches.

I just hoped the vet wasn't a man.

We had to wait in the car, all three of us, for the appointment.
They said there would be a wait and they apologized.
A mother - a human mother - and her two boys walked by our car.
She was holding a dog harness, that was all.
They stopped in the parking lot, faced each other in a triangle
with round edges,
and began hugging each other;

mom and older son, mom and younger son, son and son.
Then they got in the car and drove off.

The vet was ready for us.
He was a man.

Life in Color

Life does not fall onto pages;
there is no book of life.

But there is a tapestry of
life. We each have a thread -

not each person but each soul.
And the threads are different colors;

the grays and black stand out.
The boring are colorful. They

all come together, for better
or worse. Only the dead know

the image the threads create -
or maybe it is a single word.

The dead see it, then they are living
once more and more forgetful than before.

I think I remember seeing a dagger -
or maybe it was a cross. There was something;

a centerpiece. I saw my part in the tapestry,
but I cannot remember the color of my thread.

I just know the tapestry exists, as do you, and that
our corpses formulate the greatest piece of art in the universe.

I also know, as do you, that this ugly population
is only skin and bones - there is no spirit here.

When I

When I wake up with crud in the corner of my eyes and a damp layer of sweat

I know last night is too far in the past, too far below ground for anyone

to dig up and salvage.

When I take out two slices of bread, spread the mayo, lay down the deli meat,
lay down the cheese, and wrap the tinfoil, I know I won't be hungry.
I may force it down, or I may close my eyes and try to remember last night.

When I pull into work and take my last breath for eight hours, I return to the body
of my four-year-old self and cry that my belly aches. But no one comes to
my aid and all the medicine is at my apartment.

When I sit down at my desk, I fall weightlessly into the pit of the Earth and see

the early 19th century miners - only the whites of their eyes - who offer

familiar looks empty of any hope.

When it is lunch time I look forward to dinner. When dinner comes I regret the

price. I never eat breakfast. My own flesh has lost flavor - plus there isn't
much left ever since the vultures came.

When the end of the day comes - it comes sooner each day - tomorrow is too much
and for a moment my car doesn't start. Then the engine sputters and I have
to start the cycle once more.

When I realize each accomplishment is the start of a single-lane road that runs through
the horizon, I start to wonder what it is like beneath the pavement. Then I remember
that I have a car - but no gasoline.

When I talk to my parents and my father says, "Everyone does it; you have time to do what
you want on the weekends and at night," I take to the laptop when the sun is down
and realize that there will never be enough time.

When I write this poem - at night on a Monday with a full(?) week ahead - the last line
evades me, even when I search my day, but I find the answer by escaping the
question.

Somewhere In My Industrial Soul

When will the great wave crash down
on me? I want to shiver beneath that mountain,
forget about the summit,
hold my breath,
and be filled with pages from Poe;
then these poems would float
and I would never drown,
and the doors would never close;
I would forget the darkness of the closet
and come into the light wearing a pearl-white silk robe.

But there are droughts all along the west coast,
a place I have never been,
so I cannot be sure where the rest of the droughts are,
and how many there are.

I think there is one
where I reside in time, where ever that may be.
Or another ice age;
I cannot move and I am not sure of the cause,
and I cannot say I feel different.

This is where I am:
somewhere with shattered glass
and the smell of burning flesh.

Sacred Scribbles

Isn't this what they all want:
a blood-speckled face and round,
tired eyes. Perhaps I am too close
to the mirror.

They listen to fake families
and taboo columns. I am
looking for guidance and
listening for silence.

How the winds turn,
in and out,
leaving a thin wisp of nothingness
between the vortex.

That is where peace resides
budding with mediocrity,
shunning me like an 18th-century whore.

Past lives are real
else we wouldn't have history.
In my past life, I was an abused housewife
who scribbled poetry while the baby slept and
her husband was at work.

This one is for you,
dear,
I will write your poems now.

Too Many Questions

What if it is too late for the crows to fly
and the geese lost their sense of direction
and the pigeons developed a taste for squirrel flesh,
or some other small animal,
instead of picking through the trash?

What if I looked at the birds as a child
and envied how they only stayed on the ground for awhile
before they left for the sky,
simply because they can,
and I saw these birds,
analyzed them,
what if they changed their ways?

Who would I be?
Who am I on the coldest of winter days?

I am a man without a bird feeder on those days
and on every other day.
But I have a pantry and a fridge -
even dog food.
Meanwhile, the birds starve -
at least I think they do
because I don't see them eat.

It is winter now and the keyboard is chilled,
and the birds are elsewhere
or nowhere at all.

I am here,
on the couch,
not flying.

An Unassigned Mystery

Madness is at each strip mall, each kiosk,
and each group of upright and left-looking
slugs, wobbling with a stub leg, or no left
brain at all. Madness is the wait behind
someone with their kids that run like stray
animals, waiting for a meal, but you don't
want to wait in line, so then there is the sit-
down joint where you wait to order, then wait
for your food, and you - reader - you have to
wait until I am finished with my raised-chin
complaint, a complaint that seems high and
snobby, but in reality is low as the murderer
on the run, or the dead homeless man, or the
men who kill homeless men and dogs; that is
what churns in my stomach; it is thick like a
mixture of butter and semen - lovely. And it
sticks to the bottom of my shoes, and the bottom
of my throat - all hot and boiling - slowing down
my steps and swallows that harness my murderous
thoughts - our murderous thoughts - as we slink
through mall traffic with my girl, who knows to
stray from the crowd like a beaten homeless dog.
We walk along and within the rest, trying not to
breathe or scream, wondering why the rest are
silent; or worse, talking to each other quietly.

I Think I Heard Something - Maybe a Whisper

The secret a long night holds in its frigid womb;
that secret is with me now; it is the peace of a
moment too numb to realize, plain as could be;
crumbling away like dead skin, but skin heals;
though this may be terminal, there are some
good hours; the secret is lazy eyes and tapping
fingers, like a deformed toddler, drunk off
breast milk, stumbling to its death down a flight
of stairs; because there is no difference for anyone
else besides a few when a child dies; the same goes
for everyone else and their few followers; no one
matters; that is what I realize at night, with my
wire-eyes and dumb grin; that is the secret.

Be Glad

Just be glad that the night comes
and brings darkness along;
that the day eventually ends -
or never even begins -
and it is not always day and
we are not always holograms with
fragile feelings stampeding through
codes and invisible wires and cancer.

Be glad for your first drink and
the second and the
    distorted
perception that you learn to love,
even die for -
or something else;
be glad
you can die for something
and not from a lack of something.

Be glad there our spirits in our hollow chests
and in the sky, written in the sky,
written in books bound by human skin,
and available for purchase in stores.

Be glad that, with all
the liabilities of life and lineage,
you can breathe, even if you have to remind yourself to,
even if it is medically assisted -

there is no shame in living,
but it is so damn embarrassing.

But,
be glad,
you aren't dead;
at least now you can
defend yourself
and try
to justify each breath.

Maps in the Wind

It all
comes
to you
at
once;
flys become
    landlocked,
spiders die
in the cold,
dogs forget
to bark,
cats scale
suburban houses
and city apartments
to the roof
and meet each
other on the
ground.

It comes
at once -
too quick
to define
and
too
hostile
to hogtie.

It comes
with all
the answers
and
forgotten manuscripts
of the past
in its trunk,
but it
can never
remember
    your address -

now that you
think about it,
you only
know
the way
home,
you don't
know
the address
either.

Invisible Summit

Oh,
    invisible
mountain top, your
takers have been
        writers and prostitutes and drunks
        and bad fathers and friends of the paranormal.

    Your
summit is blu rred from

my perspective.
The hills
    and
        endless
            bounds,

my bare feet
                    and naked heart,
we all cry together.

Mountainous
                        synergy fills
the air of us all,
                    slowly slipping into
defeat then
                    giving in because I
am not meant to
                be a taker of yours; I don't

have the proper shoes

and I didn't bring

anything to eat.

It is a beautiful defeat because it is

unheard and unseen.

Prayers

No God to pray to when I stub my toe,
and no one that will listen -
or that I want to hear my sorrow -
to my slight groans and flickering eyelids.

Where is that being - or non-being -
for the woman on the street corner
and the 16-year-old butcher?

Maybe they have been doing research.
Maybe they decided there is no solution for us;
we are oil in the eternal water of life.

Too many voices claiming to be holy,
crawling around my prune-like brain,
all biting like ticks.

There is no God to pray to,
but there is the sleeping dog on the couch
and warm take-out food,
and the perfect drunk,
and the calming high -
these things are more God than anything or anyone
ever written or spoken of,
because people pray to them
far more than they pray to God.

Sometimes,
they even answer
our prayers.

Not Scientific or Factual

All we do is nod off
beneath the sun's light,
the same sun that rained down
on the Nina, confused men ready to
confuse others, ravage them, and distort
their minds further in the process,
the ship bobbing against its will.

Are we nodding or are we melting?
There is still the sun and then there is
a torn ozone, as well as impending doom,
but are we shaking our heads yes to this?
Are we accepting, or have we lost our will?
What did we have instilled in us from the beginning?
We want to know where our meat came from,
where the whiskey was distilled, where the
minuscule gem on your ring came from and how
long it was there, who bred the dog and whether their
parents were champions or hunters,
but we don't care what is in us,
or perhaps we forgot to care.

It is both:
we are nodding yes to what was - though we
never saw it - and nodding yes to what is next,
though we are unsure what that may be.
We are melting too; melting from the combination
of closing walls and an ever-increasing village.

Melting, even in the dead of winter, our spoiled
souls boil against our ribcages and inflame our lungs.

We are melting and we will continue to melt, even
with every Green New Deal and protest and political part,
we will melt; we crossed the threshold with the invention
of anatomy: skin, bones, and organs. Then came
consciousness and we went up in flames.

Icicles

The coldest days
and the hottest
amount to equal
misery.

On the coldest day
of the winter -
thus far -
the homeless man
on the corner of
Herald and
North Clinton
was there
like every other
day.

He had on
snow pants
a thick jacket
gloves
and a winter hat.

A street away
I was having a
depressive fit
in my
heated
apartment;
about work

or writing
or something.

I thought
of the
homeless man
on the corner;
where did he
get his clothes?
Where are
the donors
now?
Who am I,
but everything
that exists
without a soul
bound by skin?

The next day
I felt better
and
he was still
on the corner
full of
the soul
absent
from my car.

Enough

So,
all
I have
now
are
the words;
the cycle
of every day,
every year,
every retirement,
every funeral.

These words
don't
even
ensure
a funeral,
only
a brief
whisper
of sanity
from my
fingertips
to my
chest,
then it
spirals
like a drain
to

my feet,
where
the sanity stays;
just enough
to
wake up
each
morning.

www.ingramcontent.com/pod-product-compliance
Lightning Source LLC
Chambersburg PA
CBHW022201160726
48282CB00024B/274
* 9 7 8 8 1 9 6 2 0 2 6 2 0 *